The Pure Inconstancy of Grace

THE pure inconstancy of grace

RICHARD ST. JOHN

Originally published 2005 by Truman State University Press, Kirksville, Missouri.

Reprint edition, 2021, by the author.

Cover art: Kate Wattson, *Brown Bag*, oil on canvas, 1999. Reproduced courtesy: www.bddingtons.com

Cover design: Teresa Wheeler
Type: Adobe Garamond Pro, copyright Adobe Systems, Inc.; LegacSanITC, copyright URW software.

Library of Congress Cataloging-in-Publication Data
(for the 2005 edition)

St. John, Richard, 1952-
The pure inconstancy of grace / Richard St. John.
    pages cm. — (New odyssey series)
ISBN 1-931112-49-5 (alk. paper)
I. Title. II. Series
PS3619.T249P87 2005
811'.6—dc22

                                                    2005011593

ISBN for reprint edition: 978-1-0879-6639-7

*With heartfelt thanks
to the family, friends, and fellow poets
who have supported me
along the way.*

Contents

Acknowledgments

Special thanks to the editors and staff of the periodicals in which these poems have appeared, sometimes in different versions:

Carolina Quarterly: "Epiphany at the Dennis Public Dump"

The Comstock Review: "From the Plate"

5 a.m.: "Heidegger's Pear"

HEArt: "L'Anima Semplicetta"

Meridian Anthology of Contemporary Poetry: "All Souls Flight" and "For a Friend a Friend Turning Thirty"

Paper Street: "The Sainthood of St. Julian"

The Sewanee Review: "A Largo"

TPQ OnLine: "Walking with the Lady With Three Dogs"

yawp: "The Bird in Our Garage" and "Photographs, Circa the Present"

HEIDEGGER'S PEAR

Heidegger's Pear

Imagine a pear. First, its freckled, golden
surface, then the freckles softening
to oozy spots of brown. The pear's dissolution
not a thing that happens to a pear, but one
with its very being, with it from the first
green node upon the stem. But, unlike man,
the pear cannot imagine
what its death might mean: not just
a world without the fragrance
of this one pear—gone. Not just
a world without the fizzy orchards
leafing out in spring. The possibility—
the shock—of not-a-world-at-all,
and no one to imagine one again.
The possibility that signifies "the measureless
impossibility" of anything—the absent
dark, dark soil, from which
these fragile blossoms grow.

Banding

Apart on our 26th anniversary

This is what we must learn
over and over: Every footstep
in the mown catch-lanes
marks the frost dark. The dew
is heavy in the mist-nets.
We can see our breath.

That the catbirds struggle.
The grosbeaks bite. The finches
and magnolia warblers
are docile in the net.

And how to disengage them
from the close, black mesh—
wing first? foot first?

When to still them, when
to let them flail. And how
the junco's arrival signals
the end of fall migration.
That many, many fail
on their long journeys. Yet how
unstoppable their call.

The silver bands, that wholly
unique enumeration, script
engraved so small it can't
be read in flight, but only when
at last their bodies fall.

That our imperfect knowing,
these crude notations
penciled in a form—species, sex,
hatch-year, band—may make
some difference at another time.

How after it all—the handling,
the weighing cone, dumped
through the plexiglass slide, tumbling
and turned un-right—the birds
still take their ready flight.

And may we learn
what can't be known:
this one warbler,
heart beating, on its back
in this cupped palm.

Praying in the Dark, Age 50

My beloved is like a gazelle...
—Song of Songs 2:9

I

I sit in the dark. It is almost
our anniversary. I hold the skull
of a deer my wife brought home.

Make no mistake, this
is where we're going:
the pristine bone,
the empty brain case,
the jaw half gone.

One light branch
of antler in each hand,
I follow it down.

The shattered nose
sniffs along the ground.
The enormous sockets,
vacant and round,
my only vision.

We pick our way
across invisible
wet snow, dark deer-runs
arched with bramble
along a shaley hill.

We clamber
a black culvert,

down and down,
through fissures, crevices
where only water goes,
down rock, through stone.

We've reached the end,
the black and lapidary
heart of things.

II

I loose the antlers now
and cradle the empty vessel
that you brought.
The darkness here
is almost intimate.

I run my hands along
the four tectonic plates
of foreskull, feel
the stitch-like line
of pinholes where they join.

Along the half-jaw left, the teeth
are oddly loose and light,
like maize. Inside
the skull case, something
flickers like black flame.

I sit in silence. The deep earth
shifts and breathes.
Bedrock, fittedness.
I follow unseen water down.
I kiss you in the dark. I drink.

All Saints Eve

Listen to the voices of your dear dead relatives and friends,
beseeching you and saying, "Pity us, pity us. We are in dire
torment from which you can redeem us for a pittance."
   —John Tetzel, *Vendor of Indulgences*

Indulgences are pernicious because they induce complacency....
Man must first cry out that there is no health in him. This is the
pain of purgatory. I do not know where it is located, but I do
know that it can be experienced in this life.
   —Martin Luther, *Synopsis from the 95 Theses,*
      October 31, 1517

This is the night the dead are out. I am searching
the streets of Blawnox, past the boarded machine shops
and the darkened marble works. I am looking
for a gray Chevrolet—the car my father talked about
to say why we must always tell the truth.
He had cruised with friends one Halloween
and a gray car just like theirs was seen
speeding from a robbery. Police had come
while he was gone. His mother had to know for sure
that he was innocent. My headlights catch
some crumpled candy wrappers in the weeds.
A cracked mask flares up white. I hear
the starlings gathered in the trusswork
of the darkened bridge. And there it is—
or may be—pulled beneath the underpass.

The car door sticks, but opens. The dash
gives everything an eerie underlight. I can't quite
make him out, slouched there opposite. We sit
in silence and I smell—in memory or now?—
his smell, his smoky clothes, a tinge of alcohol.

I think of how one time he came home late,
his nose bandaged, a nasty gash
above one eye. He said that he'd been looking
at the moon. My mother didn't say a thing. I went out
in my pajamas and stared at the crumpled fender.

The pale illuminated skin on everything, my hand,
the frayed upholstery, is like the moon
as seen from childhood. The moon across night snow.
Imagined, buried by neglect, beneath that snow:
my saw blade with a plastic handle. But real
one afternoon: a little line of blood, our hobbling dog
that yelped and bit its paw. My father bandaged it.
"Cut by an icicle," he'd assumed, and maybe he was right.
Still, I found the saw that spring, in the snow melt, lying
on long grass, speckled with what looked like rust.

What has he come to say, this night
of bones and false indulgences? We sit,
a dark congruence, illuminated only
by the glow of the stilled speedometer. The mute O
of the other gauges. Distance. Fuel.
O, what is there to hide
from one another? What is there to fear?
We have said nothing. But we have shared,
at least, a truth we know, this gray
relic by the bridge abutment. The latch catches
as I slide out. And taking the benediction
of the dashboard lights, we leave by our separate doors.

Epiphany at the Dennis Public Dump

I

My father used to swing me from the muddy
shallows of the crabbing pond to its shallow
muddy bar. And help me heave the fish head,
twice as big as a man's heart, out its twine-length
in a prefect arc. I'd wait chest-deep
in the dark brown water, feeling the pulse
of current on my line. I loved him.

Wary, but not too wary to tow away
contraband half again their size, the crabs
never escaped him. Out his long pole
they lashed green-blue and lifted
in the dripping net. I'd hear their lean claws
clicking later, stacked in our dark
bushel basket under some day's dark news.

II

The rutting air conditioners
have stopped. And every light is out
this side of Newark.

No one can get off
phallic Manhattan:
Confounded at intersections,
caught this hot night
from Battery to Bronx balls.

People drag booty
through the smashed grate
of an appliance store.
Refrigerators, coffeemakers,

1200-watt hair dryers.
They come back for more.

Sunday 6 a.m. The sun
is breaking on the Hudson.
And in the turbines at Con Edison,
the blades at last begin to turn.

III

Often unholy Jerusalem,
God put his heart, his toughest
muscle in your law: The matted yearlings
humping in the pastures. The grain
risked at planting, cleaving
through time into sheaves.
No field was ever to be
stripped bare. The poor had rights
to what they found there, all
they could carry in hand.
Every seventh day, all creatures
of burden were loosened.
The turn of the grist-wheel
ceased. Even the screws
of the winepress were released.
Every seventh year, the land itself
earned rest, turned up fallow;
slaves were freed. And the Jubilee
canceled all debts. Everyone danced
the day God's ark returned.
Illiterate soldiers; the watchmen
at the parapets; David
himself, hopping at the head
of his throng. The city opened up
its gates. Paupers jammed its walls
for a view. Yahweh's voltage
coursed through the city—as Uzzah,

his tongue choked down his black
proud throat, well knew.

IV

Shadows lengthen and rats begin to venture out
on this mountain of refuse: the intimate
odds and ends of our proud seacoast.
Lines of orange flame flicker in the dusk.

The seagulls wheel gracefully above
the Dennis Public Dump. Up close,
they scrap for morsels, scruffy and fat.

From the back of my pickup, I lug and dump
our contribution: two brown bags
I'm obliged to hug to my chest.

The wind blows, but no spirit resurrects
the empty crab shells we tore apart
for dinner, or the rank fish heads we used
for bait. No holy voltage falls, either.

Only the judgment of cause and effect. Only
your good law of combustion, spreading
its pale net over the landscape.

The fish heads lie still, in their fouled twine.
I spit. I hear the hiss. I watch
the even flame in the deepening dark.

My heart has milk-blue eyes, a blind
opening to its jaws, and a rope
up its throat. *Heave it again*, you say,
in the dark water. So be it. Amen.

J. Paul Getty at Forest Lawn

Your intricate will has brought you here
to this cold storage locker at Forest Lawn.
This stark white room the end of a year
that you had hoped would never end. Now, embalmed
and scrubbed, your hair combed back, on one of these
identical chrome carts, you lie along
with every indigent in north Los Angeles.

They're waiting to be claimed. But you, Paul, wait
while lawyers clear your burial request
through city zoning channels—indignities the great
are subject to. But with luck, and the best
counsel in California, you may be allowed
your final wish: to be your own dead guest
at the knockoff Roman villa you'd endowed.

Such giving had its place; it wasn't hard.
You felt that business should support the arts.
And so it went, the limo down to Wilshire Boulevard,
your phones already ringing in the dark,
your drowsy aides, your cigarettes, the planned
meeting in Brussels, your pumping oil rigs, your heart,
your endless memos in that cramped and driven hand.

And so it went with us: We worked. We chose
unwittingly the lives that we became. Our views
were honest, by our lights. We mostly did those
things we thought we should, never made the news,
had built-in sprinklers and freshly-sodded lots.
Our kids would sign our names for gas and cruise
two exits down from East L.A. and Watts.

You wanted to be buried with the old
masters. They line your darkened galleries,
beyond the realm of being bought and sold,
this cool spring night. There's a kind of peace
about the place: the faintest starlight among all
those resurrections and nativities,
the watchman's distant footsteps down a hall.

You can have yourself buried anywhere,
but you can't just move your heart so easily.
Patron or not, no matter how hard you stare
at the gold in those medieval icons, you won't see
the firmament. Or in a moment understand
your room of Spanish mystics: how oils can be
a medium of grace, as they are for Zurbarán.

And so, the pale old man that shadows each of us,
you rest beneath fluorescent lights, eyes closed,
beside a girl found upright on a city bus
and a young streetfighter from the barrios.
Poor now, Paul, possessor of a cart, some gauze,
a rubber block behind your head, you lie reposed,
hands folded on the sheets, your nails grown out like claws.

Two Stories

Every so many years, somebody's daddy
pokes his way up through the sod.
He's just tired of it all: the pressure
of earth upon him, whole decades spent
without the slightest movement. But after
clicking his heels in the light and cartwheeling
down the street of Fond Remembrance, he slips
back home—passing through the brickwork,
through the lath—and it's the same old
stack of unwashed dishes in the sink. He goes
to work: the same sprawled papers on his desk.
Just the things he'd once hoped death
would free him from.

When he was young—
well, younger, early middle-age—
he'd had this fantasy. He'd dream
he was a kid again, a little lost but promising,
and someone would appear, a stern,
but wise old man, to take him under wing.
Then, through a regimen of exercise
and disciplined odd jobs and study of the Tao,
he'd gain, at last, that old man's focused
but forgetful grace, an ease of movement:
outward, balanced, calm.

But now,
the overcast gray clouds weigh heavily on him.
He scans the bleak horizon and he finds
no opening: just February sky, the muddy grass,
the pockmarked parking lot around the Super 8.
A kid by the dumpster in the back

swings at the feeding sparrows with a stick
and clubs one down. It's dazed. The boy,
too small for the letter jacket that he wears,
starts kicking it. "Hey," the man hollers,
leaping the guardrail at an easy gait.
"Hey, you little fucker, cut that out."

A Baptism

Some accounts say the sky "tore open." But in Verrocchio's *Baptism*
we get only these ridiculous, disembodied hands,
releasing a stylized, downward-pointing dove. It's said
that Verraccio abandoned painting altogether when he saw
how Leonardo's angel, detailed as apprentice-work
in the foreground, outshone his. Still, it's Verraccio's angel
that attracts me: halo pushed back like a truant child's;
its snub-nosed, pugnacious air, as if it already begrudged
the easy, offhand genius that would appear
throughout DaVinci's notebooks: hydraulic diagrams, flying wings,
the sketches of a forearm or an infant in the womb.

A friend told me how once he visited the maternity hospital,
but the child he'd come to see was in intensive care.
So they led him down a bright, scrubbed corridor
to a row of four small, metal-latticed cribs and one ribbed rocking
     chair.
Two of the babies lay there fast asleep and two were uttering
hoarsely crinkled little cries. The nurse explained that this was home
to the abandoned infants and put one in his hands
and left him there to rock it for a while. It was wrapped tight
in a white fleece blanket, and he said he noticed first
the startling heat that rose like a nimbus from its head, in waves.
He felt its unformed ribs move softly, out and in.
Its compact shape, its curve of spine, its utterly specific weight
seemed to take on the contours of his arm, or maybe it was
the other way around. And as he rocked, it seemed
that time had stopped, that he had stopped, but that the child
was hurtling away from him, on a solitary, dark trajectory
beyond all calculations. Perhaps returning, decades gone,
to trouble an easy evening on the street with friends, the twilight
sinking into deepest violet, a not-so-distant sign of fire.

For the sky *has* torn open and the telescopes have extended
their ribbed, rectangular, solar-collecting wings, telescopes
that, set above New York, could track the running lights
of flights that taxi up for takeoff in L.A.; telescopes that, focused
on this infant, mouthing its starchy cry… But they won't be
focused inward, for my friend's half-hour is up and the nurse
takes the restless baby from his hands, off on her short-staffed rounds,
and I am busy too, looking up that anecdote about Verraccio. And even
after my friend has told me the story, it's only occasionally, at night
in dreams, that I'm walking down a corridor and see—across a distance
and through glass—those straining, minute faces, not one
the least like Leonardo's angel. I see them, but my hands
are disembodied at my side. Time stops. There's only silence
and those small mouths moving, crying in the wilderness.

From the Plate

"Forget Herod, I am speaking
to you, the horrified onlookers.
You who said nothing, who
did not lift a hand. I see
the governor's uncle, the usual
committeemen, real estate brokers
with close political connections,
college kids serving them drinks,
a girl with a turquoise ribbon in her hair, poised
with her little whisk broom to sweep away
crumbs from the tablecloth—staring now at me.
Perhaps you were waiting for the messiah.
Let me say it again, no one is coming.
It has all been given to us, already,
on a plate. The gift of blood,
of heavy-lidded eyes, the miraculous thread
of optic nerve, the right and left
lobes of the brain, each turn of DNA
in each of these numbered hairs.
Enamel, dentin, root, the hard beauty
of these broken teeth, the ghost
of my breath, which (though you don't
believe it) will forgive you yet,
this swollen tongue, slashed cheek, yes everything
you need, this blood-encrusted ear."

Photographs, Circa the Present

There's no telling what will betray us.
A dated piece of furniture, a stranger's car
half cropped out of the picture.

Even posed by timeless foliage, something
will give us away, coming off the album page
as palpable and indistinct as light.

The turn of a collar, the cut of our hair.
Some tentative set to the shoulders
we're unaware has marked our generation.

Then there's the technical sphere: the witless
focus of our sonar cameras. The characteristic color
our emulsions will have in fifty years.

Format and finish. The comic obsolescence
of photography itself. One way or another,
we'll enter the dumb unreality of the past.

So, at Christmas parties, grade school picnics,
crowded on a sofa, or hauling a cooler from some car,
I look at the lens—and flash my ludicrous smile.

Circling Walden Pond

For Rev. Wayne C. Peck

I

He called it simply his experiment.
But though we try and try—our hearts ache
with trying—we find it too profound to replicate.

We walk around the pond. A breath of wind
scuffs the surface for an instant, then
it's glass again. A few, last, yellow leaves
hang doggedly as prayer flags on the trees.
We bow our heads beneath the doorframe
of the replica cabin and fall silent as we enter in.

The stillness, the clear space he made
by setting things aside, is like
the stillness of the lake, so still
there was a legend that the pond
was bottomless. A legend he proved base
by sliding out on ice with just a line and rock,
and measuring. Its depth, once mapped,
easy as any meadow we might walk.

Two teenage girls, from Richmond and Japan,
ask me to take their photo, as they stand
beside the nine granite pillars linked with chains
that mark where the cabin once had been.

Why do we come, drawn as if to find
our hearts' true north? As if Thoreau had mapped
this quiet clearing and this pond, not here
among the maples and the scattered pine,

but somewhere at the furthest reach
of our imagination, yet close as Concord.

I imagine these girls, or rather, one of them
in twenty years, sitting at a table strewn
with papers from work, bills, a shoebox jammed
with rubber-banded bundles that she should
have cleaned, the whole damn mess
of loves and entailments she can scarcely name,
and finding this photograph. It seems
to flicker in her hand, to burn,
recalling this sunny afternoon, how near
she came, in homage to a courage
we keep failing to attain.

II

A part of Walden Pond is Concord's public beach now.
Wooden steps lead down to a trucked-in strip of sand,
a metal sign with rules. For trash, some 50-gallon drums.
Thoreau would be appalled. But once
a friend of his observed: *Oh, I love Henry,*
but as for taking his arm, I would as soon
take the arm of an elm. Start letting people in,
the messy chaos comes: Kids whine on summer Saturdays
at packed concession stands. Teenage girls lie stupefied
on towels, in thrumming headphones, working
on their tans. Two sisters quarrel for a yellow bucket
filled with sand. A father tries to teach his son to swim
and as he slips away his hands, the boy, eyes closed,
who doesn't flail this time, first feels, for an instant,
the calm expanse of water under him.

III

The woman with the photo at her kitchen table—
let's say a teacher, in the end, with two girls of her own—
she's called, not to this quiet pond, but to a forest
of a different kind: those waving arms and hands
each asking to be called upon. The sumac and the hawthorn
crowd and compete. Maples and tulip trees
contend for their chance of sky. Each spring
the grasping tendrils spin themselves out
and new, sticky leaves perilously unfold.
By late fall, the ordinary drought and blight
have taken their toll, and the long sharp winter
is still to come. She picks up the photograph again,
and wonders if the leaves scattered in the sun,
and her friend—so close they'd thought they'd been
that year in high school—are only necessary casualties
of time, and the thicket of obligations and demands
just so much bracken it's best to clear away.

IV

Teachers, nurses, ministers like you all feel this way
at times, pressed and called from every side.
Yet, even in this thicket, Wayne, you help us see
the forest as a medium, the trees a space
the wind runs through. A blur of winter squall
connects them. So does the humid air
or ebbing twilight. You see the flickering seeds
that filter down; the dying leaves becoming common loam;
the moss and crusty lichen pointing to the north,
not as a single tree, but as a pattern; and the pond
reflecting these frail, oblivious forms back upon themselves
in all their mottled beauty. To you, I know, this seems
a trivial thing, the way the clarifying lens of pond imagines itself
merely to be standing still. And even in spring,

it feels beneath it, most, the weight of stones, and finds itself
distracted by the birds that wheel and cry above
and by the delicate shore grasses, rust and yellow-green,
waving in the wind their thin, querulous arms.

V

The friends who took me out to Walden
work at Harvard labs. There, in the basement
of Pierce Hall, they mix a soup of gaseous molecules
and fire lasers through—to form a combination that's so long
and so unstable, it lasts the briefest instant.
Yet, in several years, the radio astronomers,
using the spectral code they measured here, confirm
by soundings in deep space, this unexpected "X"
is out there, too. It's not as glamorous
as one might guess: a warren of computer terminals
and battered chairs, gray canisters, set prone,
wrapped with wire and taped with warning signs.
There's styrofoam packing patched to raw corners
and framing bolted on. I think that our experiments
must be like this: jury-rigged from found materials,
starting with a dim chaotic mix, a lens, a flash of light,
provisional, and yet amidst the clamoring, a trace
of something out of time, a listening in space:
the stillness of a lake, that silent, dark, expanse
supporting us. We listen, and for a moment, rest.

The Way the Spheres Must Move

The Darkened Mosaic

For Rhonda Brandon and her son, LaRue

*I am happy, and I think full of an energy, of an energy I had
despaired of. It seems to me that I have found what I wanted.
When I try to put all into a phrase, I say, "Man can embody
truth, but he cannot know it."*
　　　　　—W. B. Yeats, in a letter two weeks before his death

The night I learned your son was shot
I went past the boarded monastery, up
steep Pius Street,
past the crooked graying teeth
of houses on their Appalachian lots,
past the parents joking on the wooden stoops,
to the little asphalt playground at the top
with the city stretching out beneath.

A woman swept her walk.
Kids scuffled hockey sticks and chased the fading puck
across the pavement less by sight than sound.
A girl spun her younger brother on the twirl-a-round.
And on the swings, two boys
arched their backs and stretched,
reaching their shoe tips up
toward the twisted X's of the fence-top mesh.
On the hillside steps, some older kids hung out. The noise
of radios marked out a space for them
to talk and watch the city lights come on.

How could they play or swing or sit?
How could that woman keep on
sweeping, in the face of it?
Not just your son,

but the whole city, it seems, undone.
Kids smash the streetlights.
Trash collection's down to every other week.
Still, she sweeps
although it does no good.
She's only moving grit from place to place,
knocking a pebble loose
and scuffing the rusted reinforcement rods
exposed beneath, like bones in an x-ray scan
or, watching her sweep, like cords
across the back of her extended hand.

Maybe your son
was just the small gray knuckle of a stone
somewhere in the crumbling urban aggregate.
After all, what had he really done
at twenty-two?
A medical supply technician,
steady at the hospital, affectionate
to his fiancé and you.

And yet,
that woman bent to her broom
in the coming dark
in accord with mysteries beyond effect:
a structure or a rightness running through.
Her sweeping, and the swinging up and out
and the children spinning like the constellations
on the twirl-a-bout
all make a motion
and the motion with the structure brings,
unseen, a burnishing.

And with this burnishing, the stones
become a sprawled mosaic.
Every burnished stone a light among

the city lights spread out below.
The pale peach vapor-lamps in rows
along the highways, the moving glimmer of a bus,
the bluer streetlights coming on,
and lights of houses, every light a room,
each room an individual.
I try to picture it: a wall of inlaid fire—the whole
perfected city—but something else appears
more like a human face, like his or yours.

L'Anima Semplicetta

Dear Mr. St. John: Thank you
for thinking of me. I am fine,
though I have no words
to say how it is here. You ask
what you should do. Set down
your poem about the man who's blinded
by the smoke while climbing up
the Mount of Purgatory and about
the "simple soul." Take back
the bullet from my brain.
Pick up my schoolbooks and my hat
from the pavement. Follow
the stray shot back. When you get
to Marshall, take the gun from his hand.
And re-collect the smoke. Tell him
I'll come sometime to loose
the knot of anger from his neck. But you
must keep on walking, to my school. Climb up
its seven stone steps. And on the fourth step, sit
and weigh the flattened bullet in your hand.
It is such a light, slight thing;
and it is not. It is all the weight
of our whole world. It is what
we make. Now do something that will not
make sense: touch it to your lips—
this cold, dark coal—then set it just
beneath your tongue. Of course
it leaves a bitter taste. Let it
dissolve. Let it become your bones.
Let it cloud your brain. Let it impair
your speech. And let your tongue,
at all the worst of times, suddenly

speak the obvious. Let it never
stop speaking the obvious. Yours, Ebony.

The Way the Spheres Must Move

For John Stewart

I

Like any life, it's too much to make some statement from,
and yet we must—state, salvage. Like students
forced to memorize passages from Dante,
hating such pedantic violence to the whole
but finding years later these fragments
are all we have. Take, for instance, your last night:

You showed up at the psych-ward—for no apparent reason.
Your mother came at 2 a.m. to bring you back.
Out on Route 19, caged in that forest green
Ford Fairlane with who knows what private beasts,
you heaved the heavy door against the black wind,
the headlights homing in like suns—and jumped.

The trail ends there. It picks up where
you'd broken in some kitchen for a carving knife.
Then you'd run, short-breathed and stumbling, down
to the brown, pre-spring suburban underbrush
we shared in childhood. And with the dawn
just paling the horizon, you cut your throat.

II

At twenty-seven, you had taken off
for some Buddhist camp in Colorado,
promising to send me your address.
It never came. I tried once to phone
your parents, but there was no one home.
I let it slide a couple weeks and then they called.

You'd been back with friends in Pittsburgh for three months.
I'd missed touch. In front of your family's house,
there for the intimate, awkward, necessary talk
after the service, I had to fix a flat.
In the cold rain, my numb fingers fumbling
the tire iron, I grazed my hand against the street.

I wished that I—my grease-black knuckles,
my thin blood thinning in the rain—could have
done something for you. It wasn't guilt I felt
but a failure of love, that failure of flesh
to ever be another's flesh. I screwed on the last
two lugs from the hubcap and went inside.

    III

Love made the spheres move in Dante's scholastic
universe, so primitive, so smug—its circles,
terraces, even the angelic orders
down to a science. But what of our cosmology?
Its plate tectonics, the winding stair
of double helix, and light diffusing through expanding space?

We grew up with it. We'd met in fourth grade—
five years after *Sputnik*, when Watson and Crick
were picking up their laurels in Stockholm—
two minnows swimming a concentric shockwave
of the baby boom. As sophomore debaters,
between museum research stints, we walked
in the hulking shadows of the dinosaurs.

In this scheme you are gone with them, your time here
a parenthesis (that opened at a labor room
in flat, suburban Park Ridge, Illinois
and closed in a bloody thicket). The logic

as persuasive and immediate as today's
happenings, off the fiber optic link from UPI.

    IV

Against all that, I sense your presence
every time I cross this parklet, tucked between
museum library and parking lot. We had often
met here: cobblestones, some grass, a concrete bench.
Now, tonight, the trees toss in a sharp wind,
the parking meters, buildings loom up dark.

Who can know the architecture of a human heart?
Mine, prone to the pathetic fallacy.
Yours, as impenetrable as the events
of your last night. But sure as I know anything,
I know I loved you. I ponder this helpless fact,
here by the meters in a public park.

The planets wheel above me like a tire iron
and turn like lugs. The night is distant
as your mental illness and as dark as grace.
The buildings' silhouettes seem close as fifteen
years of friendship and palpable as death.
And I go on, across this cobbled path.

    V

The sun on purgatory mountain spun
impossibly, yet Virgil had some schoolman's
explanation: totally rational, radically wrong.
Meanwhile, Dante watched a flock of penitents
come down a slope, chanting a *Miserere*
to their Lord who had taken human form.

For a moment they stare, Dante's solid frame
a bafflement to them. And he, in turn,
perplexed by what winding, private journeys
must have brought them there. Then the shades crowd round
beseeching Dante, tired from his own climb,
to carry their names and features on.

So, at Ravenna, finished with his poem, he summons up
the shade of Buonconte: saved at the last
by a tiny tear, though his gray disfigured body,
washed up on some riverbank, was never found,
after he had run, flying on foot from the struggle
at Campaldino, wounded in the throat.

A Largo

A little like the face of God, we can't look
at music directly. And so, the woman in the yard
of her apartment block cannot explain
why she is moved so by the largo of the maple seeds
spilling from the high branches, the sun
through the leaves, scattering gold florins
across the rusty wrought iron table.
And, through the drawn, propped sash
of a courtyard window, what also flutters down:
Bach's little sarabande, the opening
clear sound of the *Goldberg Variations*.

This is still in Dresden, where as a child
her face and arm and hand were scarred.
And it was in Dresden that Count Von Kyserling,
awake another night and sweating in his sheets,
would pull the velvet braid to have young Goldberg
play his teacher's variations yet again.
And it was better after a while, the harpsichord
sometimes calming, sometimes its odd, angular exuberance
skittering away, but always coming home.
So he gave the graying Bach a golden cup
filled with gold florins and, later, a reference to the king.

It scarcely matters now, this breezy afternoon,
that Bach once thought about his three-part canons
as emblems of the Trinity, three in one
and one in three. Neither his variations,
branching and unfolding like these trees,
nor his neat theology made any lasting difference.
The bombs in their terrible obbligato tumbled from the sky.
The crescendo of flame lifted, crested, and consumed.

The fugue repeats. The Watchmaker God withdrawn,
his precise instrument, the spinet of the world, plays on.

Near sixty now, she's sitting at a table in the sun.
It's not that everything has come right in the end.
She still awakes at night, looking for lost friends
among a maze of charred foundation stones. And yet,
if God's withdrawn, he must have left behind
at least the space and form of music. Here, as figures
drift back home from work or market, taking the worn
shortcuts through the battered grass, he left
the seasons' bars and staves—the maple seeds twirl down
and, later, it will be leaves, drifting or skittering
and then, in the chill breeze, the first note
of winter, flurrying, haunting. He left
the quality of resonance and pattern. And something else—
not a watch-tick, not exactly a pulse, but something
that insistently presents itself. And even if
it's only our own voice, humming as we haltingly
try out some fragment, we pause as if to catch
if we're in tune or off. So, though she can't
speak precisely about music, or for what
the people passing by might hear or think,
she listens intently, not just to the Bach,
but to the soft scattering of voices
from the gray apartment block and to the seeds
that rustle at her feet. She turns her inward ear.
She lifts her scarred hand and, after what seems
an instant's hesitation, conducts a little in the air.

The Bird in Our Garage

Out with the garden tools, old paint and padlocks,
dwarfed by the big chest freezer and our cars,
we keep an unfledged robin in a cardboard box
covered with mesh, set on some folding chairs.

So young, we have to poke raw burger down
its gullet twice an hour, thralls to its shrill *skreek*.
Poor scruffy thing, confetti black-white-brown,
it stares up at us, and spreads its demanding beak.

Meanwhile, on our backyard hillside and beyond,
every sparrow, starling, robin but this one
lives and dies, squabbles, feeds and chatters on
without our aid, or even our attention.

For a bird, we run and get the garden gloves,
shred up the Sunday paper for its nest,
and call the vet, without once thinking of
the human miseries we read, on which it rests.

Still, here I am: toothpick in hand, poised above
the startling yellow mouth, now bending close—
my awkward parody of mother-love.
It makes me wonder which would be the worst:

for us to learn, by reason, to ignore
the heart's unreasoned promptings; or run, instead,
to get the gloves, the cardboard box, and poor
hurt bird, imagining that made us good.

Walking with the Lady with Three Dogs

I

"Airport Worker Crushed When Girder Fails; Probe Begins"
In response to a similar situation at Siloam
where a tower fell, killing eighteen, the Gospels

are none too consoling. Jesus, the press of the kingdom
hard upon him, refuses to ascribe peculiar blame
or innocence to the victims, instead concluding

change your ways or watch what falls on you. According to
the final investigative report, excessive shear loading,
alloy composition, and human error were all reviewed

as possible causes. In one exhibit, an electron microscope
shows standard carbon steel; its dense, packed structure seems
a firm assurance. Yet many orders down in scale,

each solitary nucleus, itself cohering only through
the pull of charge and countercharge, drifts light-years
from its own electrons, spinning somewhere vacant and away.

And if we consider other contingencies, the human
factor—say the regular working stiff who adds or fails
to add the furnace manganese or cobalt,

what forces, pulls, attentions, something his wife
or foreman said, one of a hundred things at home,
were working on him then?—all somehow coming down

to synapse firings and delicate electrolytes.
When you think about it, it's a wonder the world
holds together at all, things get built, our own self-

consciousness, much less a girder or a tower, doesn't fall away
to void. So, taking our own being, manganese, solidity,
and subatomic forces as a kind of gift or given,

we build electric lights, computers, municipal
investment offerings, and airports, each the end
link, in a fragile chain of multiple contingency.

II

Yet everywhere, we weld this chain into the many forms
of bondage. Airports, for instance, have their own caste system:
Black skycaps, female stewardesses, male pilots

and, on top, the privileged travelers bound in turn
for sunny enclaves in Antigua or Belize
where they fear they may be seen by locals as they are

in nightmares: consumers for whose fetishes the forests burn,
passport-holders of the occupying force, owners of
the banks and health club memberships, expensive watches,

scarves, and name brand shoes. These tourists mostly choose
to stay near the pool and the busy shops or, if they venture
down an isolated road, may feel a falling away

a loss of solidity, when they see the dusty children
and the packs of dogs and hear, from a doorway just beyond,
a woman howling like the mad. So, when Jesus says he's come

to set a fire to the earth, commands the rich
young ruler to sell all, proclaims the first as last,
his anger is justifiable. We feel the rightness of his harsh

tale about the man who passed by Lazarus, when even the dogs
would come...how in the end, Dives, Carnegie, whoever

we imagine wealthy, will find himself in fire across a vast abyss

and beg a drop of water from his Lazarus, his injured worker
or former shoe-shine boy. But the chasm of death,
which neither rich nor poor can cross, is also the gulf

between the fiery wreckage of our possibilities
and the things we might have done or built; the thirst, regret.
A business traveler thumbs through the in-flight magazine:

the self-improvement articles, the ads for plush hotels
and exercise machines. Hitting a spot of turbulence,
in the uneasy instant of that drop, he may look out

the window, touching for a moment on the thought
of his own end, as "Fourteen Killed in Airline Crash."
Hearing the instructions for approach, he hands his empty glass

to a passing stewardess, and reads again. Outside,
it's night. The orange lights of Dayton or Los Angeles
appear as tiny flames, across a vast dark gulf.

    III

The lights, from houses cobbled down the hills
of my own neighborhood, are warm and comforting.
It's the kind of place where families go by car

to Disney World or tour Old Europe through
Busch Gardens' backwards telescope: a small-scale
Lake Geneva and Mont Blanc, a Leaning Tower

and English guards in livery—so "real" you almost see
the pastel-colored countries of your grade school maps.
But who's to say they haven't seen the world,

relaxing with a beer, a sunny table and bright flowerbox,
their kids in Alpine caps, when every day the world—
its English menus, jeans, and Visa cards—is striving to become

this ersatz Old Bavaria chalet? Are we to judge
these aspirations or the modest houses on my block,
jammed plot to circumscribed front plot, and fence

to well-trimmed hedge, to Mary shrine, to chain link
fence? Each spring, the men rebuild the small retaining walls
that face the street, the cinder blocks edged out, uneven,

toward collapse. Still, market values drop. My neighbors worry
what kind of family will buy the duplex with the sign out front.
Yet, despite these forces, every Independence Day

grown children and their kids, long moved away, come back
for races on the football field of our small park.
Somehow the kids age six, like wild electrons, all line up,

unstably, and sprint across the green expanse of hope
and at the chalk line, cheer or whine or taunt
depending on their fortunes. In *Confessions*,

Augustine (veteran race-day volunteer, his megaphone in hand
against the pandemonium) observes that it's not goodness
but a lack of power that makes a crying infant

seem so innocent, small fingers fisted in a rage
and wholly self-absorbed. Later, the park's a stage
for raucous singing, broken glass, and adolescent fights

all night, all through the summer and beyond,
these generations: laborers, those workers' sons and now,
uncertain of the future, the sons of ones laid off.

IV

When steel collapsed, my neighbor got a job as guard
at Allegheny Library, one of Carnegie's first,
inspired by Colonel Anderson, who'd opened up

his study full of books to Andrew, then just a bobbin boy.
He'd endowed two thousand others by the time he died,
dedicating some in Scotland one July, while Frick

was handling the business back at Homestead Works.
Years later, an aged Carnegie headed "off to Europe now,
to play." But in his younger days, he wrote:

"Fifty K per annum... beyond this never earn.
To continue must degrade me past all hope. I will resign
at thirty-five." Now at the other end of both

big steel and big philanthropy, my neighbor Charlie
keeps the lavatories clear of bums who wash there,
makes sure that women aren't accosted in the stacks

and, against the union rules, helps check out books
for cornrowed ten-year-olds in plastic ponchos, jeans,
and Nike shoes. He says of vagrants: "Free to the People

don't mean squat, if nobody can tolerate the fumes." So he balances,
and with his pay, his wife's, his pension, manages two weeks
each summer at the shore, some savings, a redecorated second floor.

Across our little world of postage-stamp backyards,
I watched their grandkids chasing fireflies
one summer night. Up down, up down, the tiny lights

appeared and disappeared above our darkened hedge.
From carefully cupped hands, they edged them into jars
with pinholes in the foil tops. Then someone had the thought

to paint themselves fluorescent; it flickered like a movie
of our neighborhood: the jars, made home-like with a bit of grass,
the glowing faces, arms and shirts, a child's dance

and in the kitchen's stark, white light projected
something they never meant: crushed insect husks,
grisly and meaningless, on faces blankly innocent.

V

"Ought implies can," says Kant. He's right. But sometimes
with the weight and tanglement of "ought," we feel
we can't. Our brittle resolutions don't hold up.

On New Year's Eve, Newcastle-upon-Tyne, the colliers,
black from the furnace of the earth, would bear
lit coals aloft and run, with flames upon their heads,

a racecourse through the ancient town. We wish a fire
of love or clear prophetic rage would drive us likewise.
But we feel more a frenzy or a wild paralysis:

the press of Lazarus on Lazarus is inadmissible, yet not
to be dismissed, our poor, the well-fed of the world, ourselves
impoverished too, uncertain how we'd meet the kingdom, should it
    come—

proclaimed in some dung, cardboard, car-part city near San Juan,
    perhaps
the axe already laid upon the root of trees—or our own end.
We can never understand with certainty the causes—

decades of fatigue or some sharp blow—that lead
to mental illness. We watch the Lady With Three Dogs
who, even in winter, walks and walks her bundled animals

incessantly around our neighborhood. Dressed neatly,
but with too much rouge, she seems a wind-embattled bird,
withdrawn, head bowed, her tiny charges tugging her

down sidewalk and up curb. On walks, I sometimes greet her
with a word. She startles, backing like an animal in fear:
"Yes, thank you. You're a good man sir, yes sir, yes sir."

VI

In an awful shot-in-Pittsburgh film, the welder falls
only for the boss's son. By night she dances clubs,
but in her something deeper burns—bright as a star,

tight as a fist, focused as acetylene—and so she risks
her hopes in one climactic tryout for the touring ballet.
I wonder, if she'd failed, would she have practiced on,

welding by day, into the brittle bones and sprains
of middle age? Or instead have married? In Hollywood
she grasps her single dream. But here, waiting

by the baggage claim, amidst the families and businessmen,
the jostling current of urgency and obligation,
while all around, unseen, the flights go up and down

like frail trajectories of lives. Or lugging my overstuffed
bag of belongings up these steps, here in this world
of ought and limitation, what should we aspire

to build or be? Along the park, the first few streetlights
start to glimmer on. Above, a vapor trail arcs off
as, unaccountably, a plane—just wires and weight

and riveted aluminum—lays out an openhanded movement
through the air's solidity. The trees spread out their branches

for the birds, some sparrows hidden in the shifting leaves.

The Lady With Three Dogs turns down our street. Her hair
is touched with ordinary gray, not fire. Her heart
on this, a quiet evening, is probably less fearful than contrite.

Past fences, porches, flickering TVs, now lost in shadow
from the hill above, she keeps on moving through
our neighborhood, her world, pulled by her unruly loves.

The Amazing Wireless Receiver

For Carolyn Otis St. John at 95

Cat's whisker, galena crystal: dark static crackling
into music. You were nearly thirty then, tuned intently
to your headset and the copper coil you'd turned and turned

patiently as hardwood with its perfect rings. Children
will listen to any apocryphal story, yours about the fateful
New York Exposition being my favorite: "Gentlemen!

Cut the cable!" dared great-great-grandfather Otis,
perched above the awestruck crowd, atop his new invention,
"not the elevator, but the safety brake." The money

didn't stay in the family long, but you did get
photographed on the sprawling veranda of your childhood
mansion, looking eager even then, skewed on the knee

of Teddy Roosevelt, back to trade Yonkers political gossip
with your father, Mayor. It must have been later
you and your older brother sent those stupefied cats

down the dumbwaiter and, holding your breath at the edge
of formal Victorian dinners, lolled linen napkins in your laps
and snapped butter roses to the inlaid heights. A streetwise

Depression kid, my father's experience was more like
the cat's: thrust through a dark succession of foster homes,
knowing only a dank uncertainty, the grinding weights and cables

of an unseen, adult world, he came spitting, scratching,
spread-legged—into your receiving arms. Thinking back
to that evening, the crystal, the miraculous, tinny music

pulled from the dark, you say, "No one will ever hear it
just that way again." True. But, as a lovelorn adolescent
mooning round your Cape Cod breakfast club with stars

and summer talent, it's not Hermoinie Gingold and her yapping
ratlike dog, or the gravel-churning red convertible
Ben Gazarra drove that I recall, but the night I first saw

phosphorescence: live, along the line of breaking waves
as on a wire. These days, lights from the new commercial strips,
shorefront developments and roadside aqua-slides

obscure the faint, watery, quicksilver that you watched
so many August nights. Still, when conditions are right,
children from the condominiums or the solitary few

who stray from Water World, will walk the shoreline's salt-thick air,
their footsteps sinking in the dark, damp sand, and feel a flicker
of reception, as they detect the ghostly static there.

Nighthawks

Peint Peint Peint The nighthawks
swoop this April night, their arcs
are dark parabolas, traced
from someone's economics text,
the iron laws of Malthus, Smith.
They dive for insects in the ballfield lights.
Males, competing, plummet past
their hoped-for mates, then pull up sharp.
Peint Peint Above the sprinkled rooftops,
the scattering of window lights,
the stuttering TVs and human silences,
the fights. I see them barely—
skittering, caught in a turn,
a fleck of white. Diving over
and over, snatching unseen moths from space.
These covetous machines, these
curving things of grace. Over
the city skyline, the banks and conglomerates
twinkling together. Over the wedding receptions,
lingering in the little social halls, the last
of the wasted food gone cold now, the guests
getting boisterous, and spilling
into the parking lot. The teenage kids
in shadows in our park, drinking and jostling—
their own spring rites.
These skittering white flecks
over the spotlit bridges. Over
the darkened mill sites far, far
down our riverbanks. Over the brightly lit
commercial strips. But what
of the plaintive *Peint Peint Peint*
of our own hearts, arcing, plummeting,

then swooping up, caught—a fleck—
in light? Feeding to mate.
Mating to feed. So much hunger
and so brief these nights. Bright, covetous
machines. Or is it something else?
Arcing. Plummeting. Desperately
throwing itself—out, out, out,
perhaps even out of ourselves?

The Sainthood of St. Julian

In the traditional version, young Julian
is given everything: richly tooled books,
saddles, horses, hounds, falcon, title
to the estate. The boy turns vicious, caught
himself by the lust of the hunt, treasuring
the majestic stance of an eight-point buck
crumpled to its knees, the paralyzed look
of peasants, scattering like chaff in a field
before his coming hooves. By accident he kills
his parents, and afterwards he gives up all,
walks barefoot fifty years. We see him in the end,
health broken, leaning on his wizened staff.

It's December, almost dark. He's waiting
on the riverbank for the ferry. This is not
death, just a real riverbank and a real
wooden boat, far out of sight, out of hearing.
He waits. The wind cuts through his thin cloak.
From nowhere, in the ebbing light, a figure
appears, a leper, with open sores on his face
and forearms. In a whisper, curled with sour breath,
he asks to share the cloak, then for the warmth
of Julian's embrace, and last for a kiss
full on those corroded lips. It is the Christ
that Julian kisses. And the two ascend.

In another account, every detail
is the same, except that Julian, waiting
by the river, lets fall his staff, tries to warm
his hands against his rigid body. He recalls
his dead parents, his childhood friends, lost
through viciousness, through time. Even God

has left him. He almost believes he would give
it all up, his prayer, his penitence,
for a warm fire, some good wine. From nowhere
the leper comes, with nothing, even a shawl
to share, and sitting by the barefoot, hunched old man,
gives Julian that welcome, scrofulous kiss.

THIS LIGHT

This Light

For Sharry Everett

In an alcove
at St. Germain des Pres,
St. Antoine holds out,
upon the awkward platter
of his extended arm,
a tiny boy. People have scribbled
on the baby and on
St. Antoine's robe—
faint umbers, pinks, and grays—
so that the supplications
make a faded lacework
on the stone. They've taped
a big sheet of paper,
right on the chapel wall,
to hold the overflow
or keep graffiti in control.
Impious, foolish, artlessly sincere
or just illegible, it all depends
on how you look at it.
St. Antoine is looking
straight ahead.
His hair is cropped.
The little boy is bald.

On the x-rays they showed you,
the innocent black spot had grown
to a gray, uneven scribbling
across your lungs, despite
the many rounds of radiation
and varying interpretations.

You trundled with your IV stand
a frail female Diogenes,
reading the faces of the visitors
and moving on, until you reached
the vacant plate glass window
that dead-ends the hall.
A gray sky filled with snow
over an empty courtyard.
You turned around again.

I wonder, sorting my Paris slides,
what we choose
and what we're given.
I remember quarreling
often with my wife
over the camera,
seeing the same things
but framing them differently.
We stood by the fountain
in the Place de St. Michel,
hissing at each other,
with the clear water
tumbling into the basin
and the saint forever
about to slay the dragon
with his blunt, immovable
bronze sword. The slender women,
catching my longing eye,
aren't in the photos either.
And what is there—
the low stone bridges
gracing the glowing river,
a lucky sunset
on the gold dome
of L'Academie Francaise—
seems irretrievable.

Each transparency
a darkened window,
within its small white frame.
I hold one up
between my thumb and finger,
a thin white wafer,
and can't make out a thing.

We visited St. Chapelle
on a sunny day.
The boyish guards at the gates
of the Palais de Justice
randomly searched the handbags
and peered into the cars.
But, writing to you now,
I don't know how to say
what kind of sun it was.
For though the light
was beautiful, it was still
the same and distant sun
radiating through
the tall, frail ribs of stone.
Nothing was healed.
The phony relics—
a box of bones,
the crown of thorns,
some fragments
of an untrue cross—
were buried beneath us
somewhere. The story's there—
Louis the Crusader,
who needed something to show
back home, honoring his mother
with the box and then
this lacey cage of glass—
in Window 7 South. And yet

we were all moved.
The generous light poured in
through the lofty tracery
and splashed its merciful pastels
across the floor, falling equally
upon the guards, us whispering tourists,
and the corrupt glass kings.

Later, on the Quai de la Megisserie,
among the overflowing
shops and flowerstalls,
my wife had pointed out to me
a low, skewed wall of cages.
I would have missed them
in the hurry of the marketplace:
this brood of fluff-like quail,
and *coqs*, live fish in jars.
A knuckle-kneed, young goat
looked soulfully out
through the limits of its wire mesh.
He stood in a bed of wood shavings—
small curlicues still clung to his curly fur—
watching the narrow square
of street that chance had given him:
the dappled shadows
and the dirty sidewalk,
the lower third of passersby
and the occasional, terrifying
dog. I couldn't help
watching him for a while. He swayed
on the bony saplings of his legs
and I only thought later
of what he didn't see,
staring mildly at the passing
hours, of what must have been
his final days. Then

I was thinking of my wife again—
this moment, as she lingered
at a flowerstall, her face
half turned away
and bent to a spray of irises,
her dowdy jacket
catching the wind,
and the great trees
branching above us,
and her gift for showing
these things to me—
how foolish and blind
in imagination I'd been.

There was a blank square
in the Louvre, where Vermeer's
Lacemaker was on tour.
I couldn't remember the picture,
so I bought a postcard,
here on the table with our slides
and souvenirs. In all his life,
Vermeer chose maybe forty scenes
to set to canvas. This one
makes me think of you, although
you couldn't look less like
this white, Dutch girl
in perfect health, with all her hair.
But it isn't her we see,
so much as how she focuses
upon her work, and how the light
from some unseen high window
just outside the frame still seems
as if it's radiating
from her downturned face.
But let's not overly romanticize
this merchant girl.

She's wearing lace herself,
a luxury. Perhaps she's only
earning pocket money
or making a pillow for her beau.
We don't know even
if she loves her work,
though she has kept at it
for centuries. Vermeer
is silent on this.
He gives us just
this girl from Delft,
working her fabric
on a wooden block.

St. Antoine, as it turns out,
is patron of lost things.
Somebody's keys, your hair
in the comb, your breath
at 3:00 a.m., suddenly gone—
alone in the thick dark,
fumbling in panic
for your oxygen.
Or say we've lost
our way of seeing,
which is another way
of saying "grace."
So people scribble
on the prayer sheets
or buy a votive candle
for five francs and set it
in the tiered, iron rack.

You rest, these final weeks,
in your old high-ceilinged room,
with its peeling paper
and crumbling crown moldings.

Soon you'll be lost to us
and your absence will be like
those oddly disturbing
figure-ground pictures:
fish that somehow
flutter into birds, or faces
hidden within flames.
Sometimes we'll see it
without wanting to. Others
not at all. It must be
like that for you now,
watching the light's pale
rectangle, cast
from your one tall window
to the white, hand-knitted blanket
on your bed. Some days it falls
hard and fluorescent
as that x-ray screen.
Some days it's gold
and soft and still.
There's no use working at it
or wishing it an easy page
on which to write a prayer
or read an answer.
Perhaps it's the pure
inconstancy of grace—
this light—each instant new,
that frees us to begin
another version
of that half carafe
of water by your bed
and spindly wooden chair.

For a Friend Turning Thirty

I

We can learn from these Dutch still lifes
in Toledo, Ohio. In the handle of that knife
resides the weight of hundreds of others
held and set aside, seen and remembered,
rendered and rerendered, seen. It takes an eye
you don't have at eighteen to paint like this.

II

The essential thing is not that these pieces
found their way to a museum, grabbed a spot
in art history, but rather the rightness
of this light, spilling through a goblet
and onto a linen cloth; one's sense
that the curve of this pewter platter had to be.

What counted most for these Calvinists
was faithfulness—in the even grinding
of pigment on stone, in the welcome of houseguests
with cordials in the afternoon, in thanks
for the breadth of sky above a harbor—
the faithfulness of hand and heart and eye.

III

And see, the achievement here embraces
domesticity. The brushes in that greystone jar
are no more prominent than this wooden bowl
or dented kitchen spoon. This unplatonic

vision seems equally at home with fresh
cut flowers or page-ends, or with half-carved meat.

     IV

Then there's Toledo, the kind of town
we all grow up in. Famous, in a small way,
for fiberglass. Its sights familiar
as our signatures—the plastic wading pools
in our backyards, our power mowers, the glare
from off our cars on these midwestern streets.

Just blocks from the Owens Corning Tower
in a building cleaner than it ought to look,
with Bunny Bread transit benches out front
and sporting an overly-manicured lawn,
we find these works of grace—incongruous
and unexpected. And yet, undeniably, here.

The Grecian Urn Responds

Take it from me, I was plain even then,
pocked as a pimpled girl. I never said that stuff
about truth being beauty, beauty truth.
And, as for being "a friend to man,"
that's a laugh too: I was an umbrella stand
in an investment banker's flat. Now I'm gone
to landfill, propping up the concrete bays
of a car park in Suffolk. So, the poet's hand
puffs his blank stanzas with easy praise.
You think you love me, but you love the poem.

I was a vacancy—where Keats put
his deep, deep longing for permanence;
where that banker set his sodden bumbershoot;
kids hid their glassies, agates; and where once
a Greek girl, dark hair damp across her face,
would catch a mossy rivulet, then walk home
through market-stalls, past wheat, past oil I'd hold
on other days, and with a careless grace
she'd pour the water out on paving stone:
easy, clear, miraculously cold.

She might, I think, have been a citizen
of the little town that Keats imagined
empty. Heard the timbrels and the pipes begin
their actual melody, the tipsy wind-
player faking the parts he didn't know,
his friend with tambourine, sliding off the beat.
Of course they loved the music, wanted it to go
on forever. But oh, they wanted to return again,
back to that cracked and dusty town, not desolate
but full of its daily trafficking in joy and pain.

Even that heifer—the lowing animal
pulled by the priest up that lonely hill, and then
to its rattling last, blood speckling the bowl—
wasn't grim sacrifice, but the halting emblem
of a gratitude: things given and received,
the passing, human commerce of that place.
I imagine that the gods looked down and grieved.
This isn't what Keats means. Still, he portrays
the creature, even in its final hours,
singing in its fashion and wreathed in flowers.

Flowers on a windowsill in Rome
brief in the sunlight. Also by the bed:
some scribbled lines, a bowl of bloody phlegm.
I wonder now if what I should have said—
not I, but we—is this: "Truth is what comes.
Beauty is the shape we set it in."
We were a pretty pair, even back then.
I was stained and cracked. He rattled and coughed.
But something I gave him as he wrote those poems
made him call me "bride." Even I was loved.

Upstate New York, in Difficult Times

Persistent this spare orchard, the snow
here, the sun flashing off the rough rock
of the little quarry. It grows slowly, love,
by hewing. The horses harvest perfect stone.

Meditation for a Wedding

It is an irrevocable step,
like building a house in one place
and not another. Like the first phrase
in a piece of music. I remember a trip
Kate and I took, married nearly 30 years:
early April, the passing fields stubble and bare.

Two-part sonatas on the radio—
their architecture, heard, so clear
but in the making, every note unsure.
Then heavy snow. The mountains crowded close
and the roads worsened. We passed a wreck,
debated keeping on or turning back.

We reached Jim Thorpe, "the Switzerland
of Pennsylvania." Kate recalls
the beauty of it all.
But for days a cold gray band
of cloud settled on the spine of houses, tight
in the valley, above the played-out seams of anthracite.

Despite the gloom, some small front stoops displayed
their chipped blue plates and chifforobes,
childish paintings, clothes
worn thin or out of fashion now—the ways
that households must keep on imagining themselves—
set out on makeshift racks and battered shelves.

The sun broke through our last day there.
We held hands and talked
while runoff raced along an aqueduct
cut below the houses and the mountain stairs,

reading in its flowing the mysteries of place
and possibility: cleansing, destruction, grief, and grace.

I think of it often, both that sunny walk
and one longing image: what it might be like
to live there, lying each night
in one of those houses hewn from rock
and perched above that cobbled street,
with the water rushing ceaselessly beneath.

The Chokeberry and
the Mower: A Valediction

For my wife

To protect a chokeberry bush from the city mowers,
you work tall metal stakes into the ground, rocking with your weight
in the shaley strip of weeds behind the guardrail on our street.

"The birds like the berries," you explain. This care despite the fact
you'd seen, right from your office window, a crow with something
in its beak, that something, as it wheeled away, a wing.

One of your weekend trips this spring, you went to find
prothonotary warblers. Slate-winged, with glowing yellow head and
    breast,
they like to nest in cavities of trees, near water, chiefly swamps.

"Then what is one to make," one bird book reads, "of those
that choose, each season they return, the pocket of a hunting jacket
hung from a nail in a garage?" We are like them, Kate:

one house, one marriage all these years, yet one of us
certain to depart—moved by some inward cells repeating
and repeating, like a clock—on a long migration, navigating the dark

only by the contours of a half-felt coastline. While the other, waking
to a leaf-strewn, crisp fall morning and the busy
numbness of flowers, friends, memorial, begins traveling

equally, an intractable unknown. Or one of us will go
while still around: our mottled skin, brittle and thin
and featherlike, having forgotten even the closest faces

yet recalling and repeating the measures of some song,
an aimless hand brushing a wisp of hair aside, and all
the while, still mouthing that distant, generational refrain.

We joke that you have two talents: nesting and grieving.
You anticipate the same vacation every year, down to the same
inn room; eat lunch with a book at your deli table every working day

at 2:00; arrange the cans in our cupboards and shut away
your heart when you hear that yet another set of friends is moving off
South or West. So, each weekend on your walks, you watch,

relearn, how the flies shimmer on the torn blacksnake
by the path, how the leaf-blight browns the laurel, the succession
of oak or pine crowds out the little stands of buckthorn and locust.

The jays heckle the hawks away. The hawks, in turn,
silence the woods as they pass overhead. I imagine that you pause
by a field cloaked in goldenrod, yellow as the vestments

of the pope's prothonotary, for which the bird was named,
here like the moving robe of God. You seem to be grieving already
for its passing. If you leave first, it's how I will remember you.

But for now, let's be like that crow a friend described
who came each spring and then came every day, perching on her car
in the school parking lot. It would sit on the bumper and admire

the beauteous black form of a bird that appeared each day—
miraculously—on the other side of the chrome. And so it returned,
transfixed with absurd, absorbed joy, until its own time to fly away.

All Souls Flight

For my mother

Here and there, a pool of reading light.
Passengers shift pillows, try to sleep.
Near eighty, you're moving toward a place
none of us has been—Iona, Ireland:
The Book of Kells. A sole page turned
each month. *If one stayed, you say,*
you'd see it all. Where saints, birds, beasts,
fish, flowers illuminate the Celtic cross.
A place of silence, stone, and waves, and stars.

Four rows ahead, a child wails—
has been howling for an hour.
Nothing can comfort it. Its pure cry of want
makes the whole plane uneasy in its wish,
its inability to quite forgive
that raveled howl. But you think only
of the child. You go to help. You touch
the mother's shoulder with a quiet palm.
No, there's nothing you can do. You sit again.
A stewardess steps past you in the dark.

Now I imagine that you think of us, the souls
you helped bring up. Babies. Beasts.
Those years. *The Book of Kells*, and where
the manuscript breaks off. The waves
invisibly beneath you, rushing past.
You drift. You almost sleep. Headed toward morning
with that earthly keening in your ears.

Annunciations

To me it's a mystery what happened that moment
there in that broom-swept Russian orphanage,
the instant you met your new daughter,
the uncertain air and nothing else
between you. I was in Florence
climbing the stair at San Marco,
to where, in my photo, a girl I hadn't intended
is entering the frame. She steps into the space
of Fra Angelico's most famous fresco.
Her knee is bent slightly, like the angel's beside her,
its wings a stiff tracery of gold and copper,
mauve and verdigris. Her hair is dark, like yours;
her face a frown. The one arm I can see
is folded on her chest, the way that Mary's are,
covering I guess a hidden purse. Is she
with a student group and trying to keep pace
with her talky guide and hissing, wished-for friends?
Or just lagging out of sight of distant parents?

But what I wonder is, the real question
in all these Annunciations: Will she say "yes"
to the God within her? That unknown something
she might, at her best, become: just barely
a hunch, an intuition, and so ill-formed—
what a bastardish thing it looks like now. Will she say yes
to so much grief and such unfolding all in one—this day, a day
that brings with it a faintly religious feeling,
the monastic cells, the crucifixes on the walls,
but also the gift shop, the restrooms, the *piazza* of St. Mark's,
its sun too hot. She steps into this space

and brings already in her mind, the flight behind,
the longer flight to come, the movies, the delays
at customs, then the old routine back home. Will she
say yes, and harder, keep on saying yes?

Can the two embrace? The one, stiff-winged, intent,
the other so, so young and moon-faced? Come
from two such different worlds, into this
silent, deep, pictorial space with its delicate, arched
Corinthian columns, the air so still
it seems as if it waits, this foreground
and this floor so swept—immaculate
even of shadows, and the whole scene balanced
by that flat little garden to the left, at once
edged oddly with a plain plank fence and sprinkled
with those mysterious white flowers.

Christmas Requiem

He remembereth that we are dust.
In Memoriam, Thomas Peer, 12/23/01

It's the dust that interests you now
you've become it—or not. You tell us.
Meanwhile the wind grinds down
the lovely Appalachians. The gulf widens

we call the Atlantic. Meanwhile, I pass
a front-stoop fence done up for Christmastide,
one lone strand of wire, tattered
with little tufts of foil meant

as snowflakes? Reflecting
just now a surprising, late
afternoon sun. But, as Kate reminds me,
in precisely this light, the sun's

billion-year context, who
can think this anything
but comic. Take the long view:
snow, crystals, glacier, stone.

> *Prehistoric blue jay*
> *streaks its way home.*
> *Starlings' wiry gossip*
> *hidden in high trees.*
> *Down a dark passage*
> *the star-nosed mole*
> *pushes its tuberous snout.*
> *Cornfield stubble. Apples.*
> *A thin green line*
> *along a rock outcrop.*

Luminous song of the world.
"Song?" "Beautiful?" Where
did that come from? Projection?
Decoration? I remember a poem

you taught us in eighth-grade class:
Its wavering refrain: "sun moon stars rain."
We couldn't make sense of it.
And now it's you and the senseless sun, moon, stars,

rain eating away the basalt cliffs somewhere.
You didn't even want "a service," *all that*
religious crap. Yet, as we sat there
lost, heads bowed, noses buried in the purple

mimeograph of poem, hoping hoping
not to be called, you did make sense
of it, opened it up, and even now we wonder
what you saw in us, gangly and, as I said, quite lost.

Do you remember another student, Stewart,
brilliant, luminous? To me he was
but little lower than the angels. Yet I hear his voice
frail from a mattress: *The worst*

is I can't focus. I can't even read. It's all
so tenuous... so tenuous. He told me he first knew
that he was schizophrenic when, at ten,
he saw Stonewall Jackson, cresting the couch,

crashing through his living room.
Jackson's teeth were rotten, green.
You were obsessed with the Civil War, too,
tromping the muddy fields

of Gettysburg, Antietam, dragging your bulk
over the split rail fences, firing off
theories, wild stratagems. But then
you'd pause, stilled by the carnage

at some nameless hillock, and if not prayer
what was it? Surely the dead
were more than ants,
piled and twisted, here a leg torn off,

there a gaping thorax. Says Kate, my wife:
"The average life for a mammalian species
is two million years. Our time is up." A little less
than angels? You tell us.

> Tundra swans, wings beating,
> honk as they pass overhead
> in the dark. Sand washes itself:
> pepper, pale brown, off-white and amethyst.
> Beech leaves and alder leaves
> silver underneath. Tent worm nests
> wispy and luminous. Shale flakes
> and soft sedimentary rock.

I keep speaking of Kate,
like you, long since gone
from any church, her long view—
Ruskin had it too, heard

the "dreadful hammers"
of geologists, "clinking at the end
of every Bible verse"—but did I say
how the delicate line of her spine

curves into a little ridge of bones
bluish with veins? She, too, pauses
at a nameless spot
in our lovely Appalachians,

sometimes to point out
where deer have bedded down the grass,
but sometimes to recall
a bit of music, the *Enigma*

Variations, Beethoven's *Pastoral*.
A cloud opens up. Sun catches a stone.
A glint of silica—reflecting
fractal structure, math, reflecting again

Elgar's intimate, intricate enigmas
written for his friends. At the funeral home,
comforting your widow, I felt the bones
of her shoulders, high in her back,

like wings. And wasn't she thinking
no, no, no.—more like an angel
than a stone—*You are. I love.*
Something must go on.

> *Sun on a dusty road,*
> *dust on a stone. Moon,*
> *high on a hillside,*
> *caught in the branches*
> *of an aging elm. Stars*
> *hidden—all but one—*
> *behind some scudding clouds.*
> *Rain, pattering the surface of a pond*
> *and a green frog, half submerged*
> *by a broken branch,*
> *waits and doesn't move.*

We did go on, to the cemetery building,
a high wall of windows at one end,
like the great glass wall at Coventry Cathedral
but without the etched angels.

As I remember it, I stand
only half-listening to your friend
with his gloved hand on the casket.
I watch the snow

swirl beyond the glass,
precipitating out of nowhere.
It seemed to come
out of nowhere. "Why

is there not nothing?"
Heidegger asks. "And what is
this thing in man, this consciousness
about himself, his death?"

The last time I saw Stewart
he was on so many meds, it was as if
we talked through glass. So unlike
the kid—6th grade—I'd played penny-ante poker with.

The dealer calls. The deal had come to him
after a comic-catastrophic string of loss.
He shuffled the battered cards,
announced: "We're gonna play a game

called *Stewart Wins.*" By twenty-nine,
he'd played out his hand. He ran

from home one night: a brambled hillside
and a carving knife. He cut his throat.

So tenuous. It's all
so tenuous. That fragile column
of bones, cut off
from reinforcements.

Bird-light bones
slit and whistling. *It's all…*
perhaps just whistling,
whistling in the dark.

> *Crow—peers at a foil wrapper*
> *in the dirt. A diatom*
> *flowers in an algae pond*
> *or deep in a fissure of the coastal trench,*
> *edged with pinkish phosphorescent light.*
> *Mountain laurel, flowering quince,*
> *hemlock, eyebright, mint.*

Maybe it's time for a joke.
Yours were so bad: *Two guys*
are walking dogs. They see a bar
but know they can't bring pets inside.

"Watch this," the first guy says.
He puts on his shades,
follows his German Shepherd in.
The next guy does the same.

Gets stopped. "But it's my seeing-eye-dog"
he explains. "That's no seeing-eye-dog.

That's a Chihuahua." "You mean,"
he exclaims in utter disbelief

"They gave me a Chihuahua?"
So, is it a beery paradise? Or are
your once-eyes dust? Here we look
through our glasses darkly

yet—for all of it—we laugh.
Where'd that come from, that
six-pack belly laugh
you used to have?

Kate smiles at human folly, demonstrates
by stretching out her arms. Birdwatcher, lover
of this world, she looks about to fly
or to embrace. "If this, from tip to tip, is time

since earth began, then life starts at my palm—
algae, horseshoe crabs, not a single plant on land.
Mammals are a fingerprint. And man?
You wipe out human history

with one quick swipe of nail-file
at the end." The first day you were gone,
on Christmas Eve, I watched my younger sister
lean to the mirror, daub lipstick on. Her slow

doughy features, from a tripled chromosome,
looked right back at us. Serious
and full of her responsibilities that night
on altar guild, as acolyte. Her God?

Looking at the sky
we see a face, looking at the stars
we make stick-like constellations,
give them names. A game

perhaps like *Stewart Wins*, a whistling
and a hope. If it's the other way:
our face reflecting something about God,
it must be just a glimpse, a flicker,

an enigma, come to us
not in the clinking of a Bible verse,
but as a *saying*, underneath all this.
Forget what form, a word,

God in his fragile, blind, wind-battered world,
unrecognized. At the mirror, my sister's sure—
her bright red dress, the flowing robes she'll wear—
she'll be the center of the mass. Yet, making up herself,

she also makes the world. Grave with love,
she'll fold an altar cloth, she'll pass the wine.
People looking in her puffy eyes will see a kind
of enigmatic truth about themselves.

> *Woody coneflowers*
> *poke above a winter flowerbed.*
> *House sparrows stutter*
> *between the air and ground,*
> *squabbling for seed.*
> *Little hulls of snow*
> *speak themselves*
> *out of an empty sky.*
> *Upon a distant hill,*
> *spidery black trunks of trees,*
> *gray squall between, a delicate web*
> *of branches dusted white.*

Meanwhile, the decorations here
are all still up. The tattered foil
reflecting last, late sun. Neither the sun
center of a universe, nor the comic little stars

just switched on around this window.
A little dog yaps behind a chain-link fence—
somebody's limit, somebody's home—
certain that its bark is heard

throughout the neighborhood. It wears
a joke of a red wool jacket,
knitted for it by someone. *So,* can *you get in
with just a Chihuahua?* I'm saying yes.

Notes

"All Saints Eve": Blawnox is a working-class river-town just outside of Pittsburgh, Pennsylvania.

"Epiphany at the Dennis Public Dump": Uzzah died while attempting to protect the Ark of the Covenant from touching the ground. In one interpretation, the reason for his death was pride—the belief that his hand was purer than the ordinary earth.

"J. Paul Getty at Forest Lawn": The narrative germ of this poem came from an anecdote of a friend who claimed to have worked at Forest Lawn Cemetery. No biographical accuracy is claimed. I have fictionalized liberally.

"Two Stories": Thanks to poet Michael Wurster for the poem's first line as a starting point.

"Circling Walden Pond": Thanks to my friends Carl and Elaine Gottlieb, both scientists at Harvard University.

"The Darkened Mosaic": Rhonda Brandon is a colleague in community development. Her son was killed accidentally, in a drive-by shooting, as he returned home from work.

"L'Anima Semplicetta": The title, which translates as "the simple soul," is taken from *Purgatorio XVI*. The speaker is told to sit on the fourth step, or terrace, of "love defective." The poem honors a young girl, Ebony Patterson, killed by a schoolmate in the Homewood neighborhood of Pittsburgh.

"Nighthawks": "Covetous machines" is taken from John Ruskin's series of essays, *Unto This Last*.

"A Largo": Bach's *Goldberg Variations* were named for his student, Goldberg, who went on to play harpsichord for Count Von Kyserling. The Count subsequently commissioned variations from Bach, as music to ease him into sleep.

"This Light": Sharry Everett was a radiant African-American woman and an advocate for civil rights throughout her life. She was dying at the time I returned from a twentieth anniversary trip to Paris with my wife.

"All Souls Flight": "The manuscript breaks off" in the farewell discourse of the Gospel of St. John.

"Christmas Requiem": The poem is addressed to Thomas Peer, an English teacher who helped introduce me to poetry. He died just before Christmas. Kate's description of the geologic timeline is drawn from John McPhee's *Annals of the Former World*.

About the Author

Richard St. John is executive director of Conversations for Common Wealth, a program of the Community House Learning Center. In 2002, following twenty years in community development, St. John completed a midcareer Loeb Fellowship at Harvard University. He earned his master's in English at the University of Virginia, and his bachelor's degree at Princeton University. He lives in Pittsburgh, Pennsylvania, with his wife, Kate.